Name _____

Look at the picture. With a brown crayo_____ ____s
that are alike. Color the rest of the pictu_____ _rs.

FS-2651   Pre-School Workbook-Book One

Connect the dots from 1 to 3.

Fred needs something!

Color the picture that comes first.

Cut out the shapes. Paste them in the right places.

Name _____

Follow the path to the carrots.

Skill: Eye-hand coordination

5

Name _____

Look at Farmer Fred's hens. Color the hens that are alike.

6

Name _____

Use a red crayon. Find the right path. It will take you into the cage of a zoo animal.

FS-2651 Pre-School Workbook-Book One

Name _____

Look at each row. Color the pictures that are different from the first one.

Connect the dots from 1 to 5.

• 2

4•

What do
they see?

•5

1•

• 3

FS-2651   Pre-School Workbook-Book One

Name _____

Cut and paste the shape that is just like the first one.

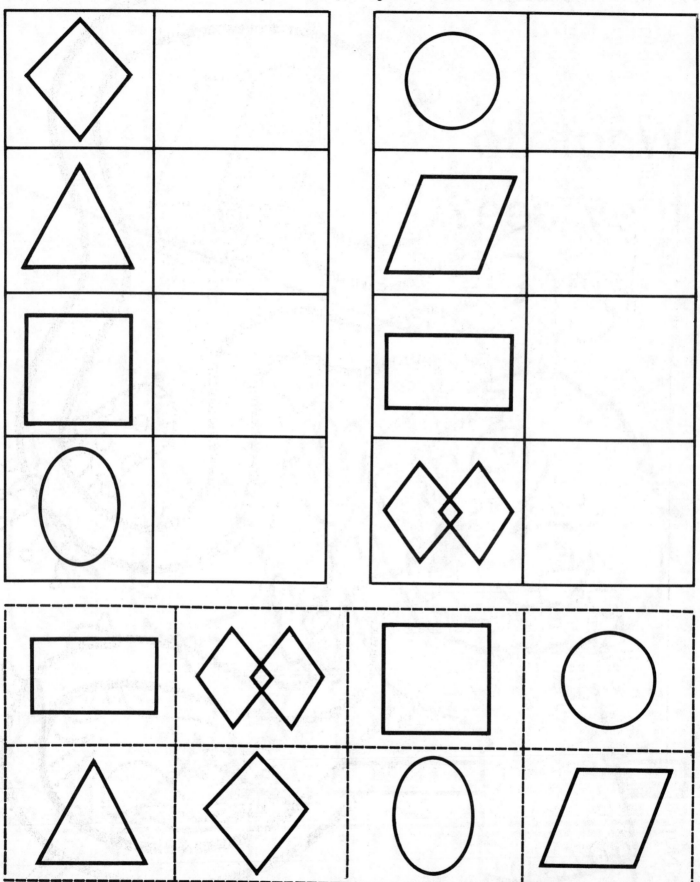

10

Follow the path to the buried treasure.

Name ——————

Cut out the shapes. Paste them in the right places.

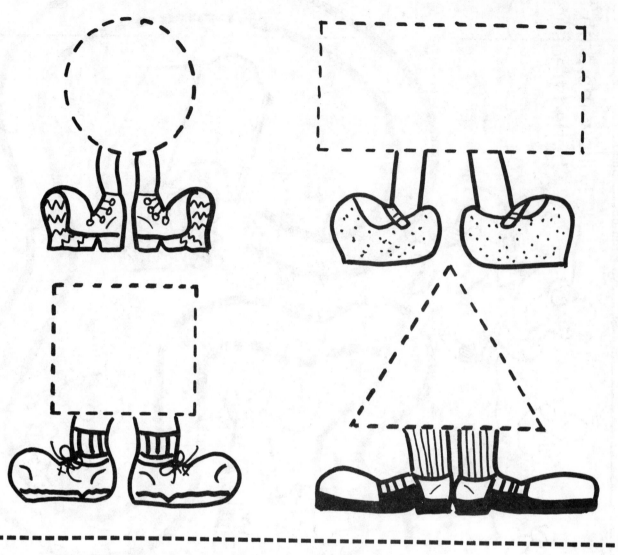

FS-2651 Pre-School Workbook-Book One

Name _____

Circle all the snakes that are the same.
Then color the snakes in your favorite colors.

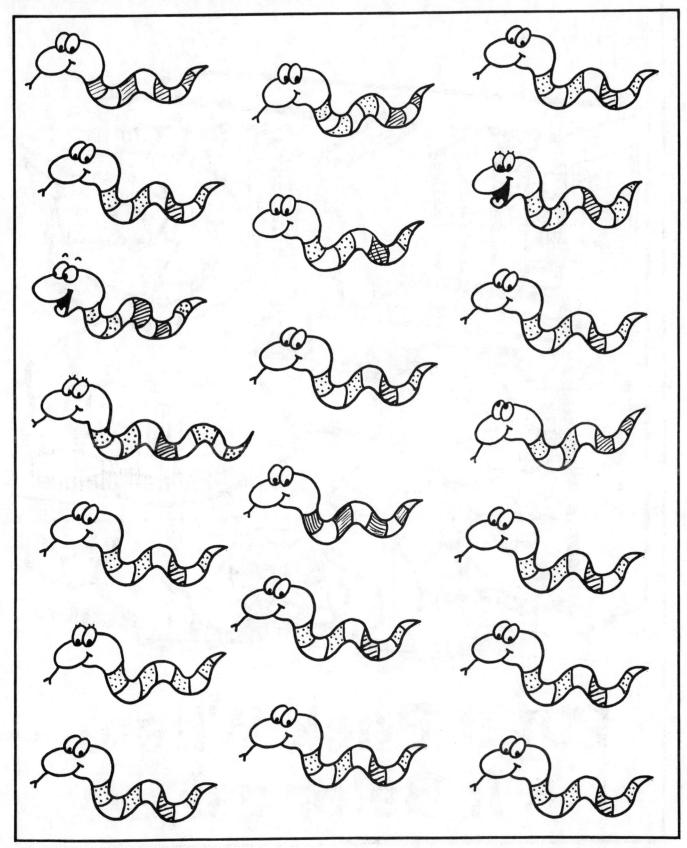

   FS-2651   Pre-School Workbook-Book One

Name _____

Color and remember.

Put It Back Where It Belongs!

14   FS-2651   Pre-School Workbook-Book One

Let the Show Begin!

With a purple crayon, follow the maze to find your seat. Be careful not to walk into the tiger cage or the monkey house.

FS-2651   Pre-School Workbook-Book One

Cover your sneeze. Color, cut and paste.

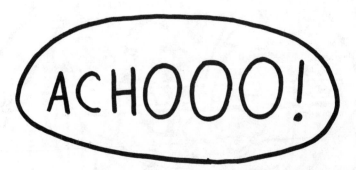

Acrobats

Color all the acrobats that look alike.

Cut and paste each twin.

Skill: Visual perception

Color everything that is alike in each row.

FS-2651   Pre-School Workbook-Book One

Name _____

Cut out the shape. Paste it in the right place.

20

Name _____

Connect the dots from 1 to 7.

Make something for Little Bear.

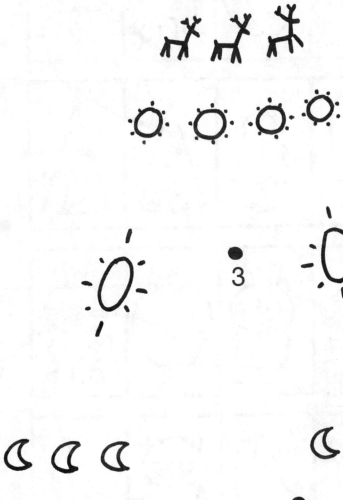

Thanks!

21

Skill: Visual perception

For each row,
color the pictures
that are **alike**.

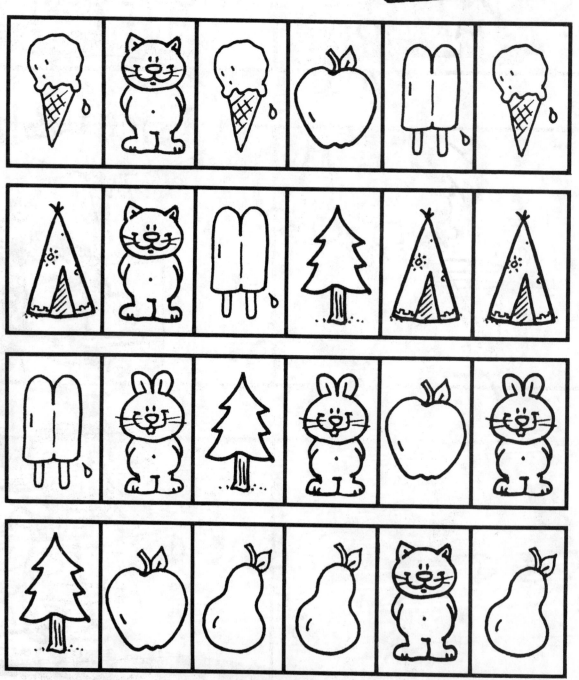

Name _____

Color the picture that comes first.

23

Name _____

Circle the three matching animals in each row.

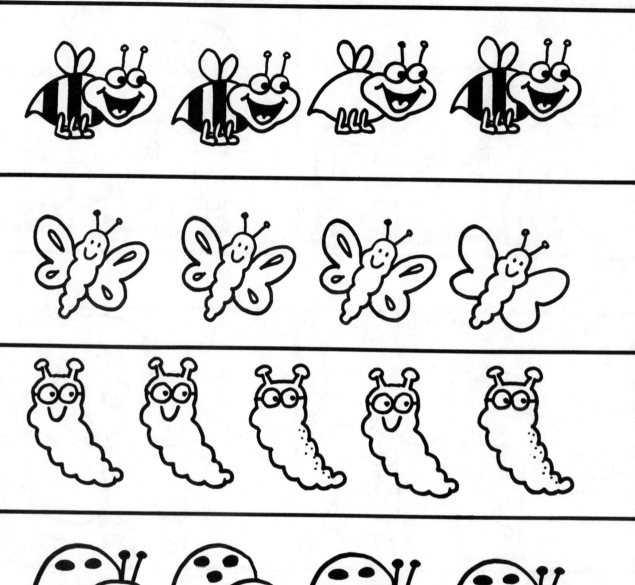

Name _____

Circle the three matching creatures in each row.

FS-2651   Pre-School Workbook-Book One

Name _____

Cut out the shapes. Paste them in the right places.

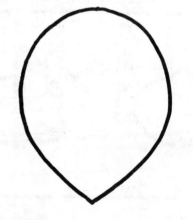
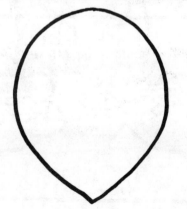

   FS-2651   Pre-School Workbook-Book One

Name _____

Follow the path to the spilt milk.

Skill: Eye-hand coordination

©Frank Schaffer Publications, Inc.   27   FS-2651   Pre-School Workbook-Book One

Name _____

Color, cut and paste.

Little Miss Muffet
Sat on a tuffet,
Eating her curds and whey.
Along came a spider
Who sat down beside her,
And frightened Miss Muffet away!

Name _____

Make them both the same.

Skill: Eye-hand coordination

29

Connect the dots from 1 to 5.

Name _____

Skill: Eye-hand coordination

Copy the space creatures!

FS-2651   Pre-School Workbook-Book One

Name _____

Color the pictures
that are **alike**.

Name

Skill: Eye-hand coordination

Follow the path to the bone.

FS-2651   Pre-School Workbook-Book One

Name _____

Cut out the shapes.
Paste them in the right places.

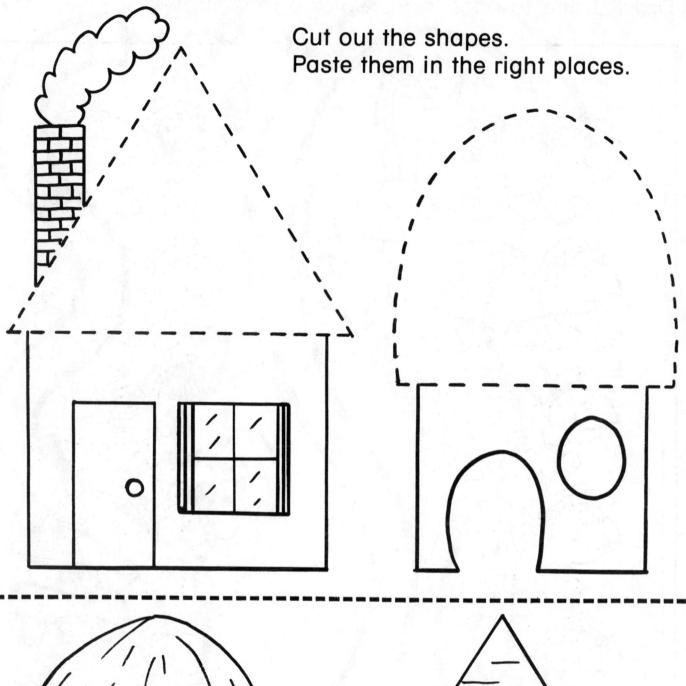

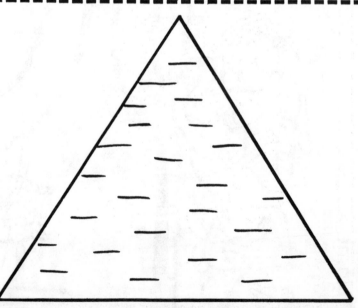

34

Draw a line to each twin. Color all the turtles.

Name _____

Connect the dots from 1 to 7.

Follow the path to the flowers.

Skill: Eye-hand coordination

FS-2651   Pre-School Workbook-Book One

Name _____   Skill: Fine motor skills

Trace over the _ _ _ lines. Color the picture.

FS-2651   Pre-School Workbook-Book One

Skill: Visual perception

Name

Circle all of the fish that look just like the one in the picture.

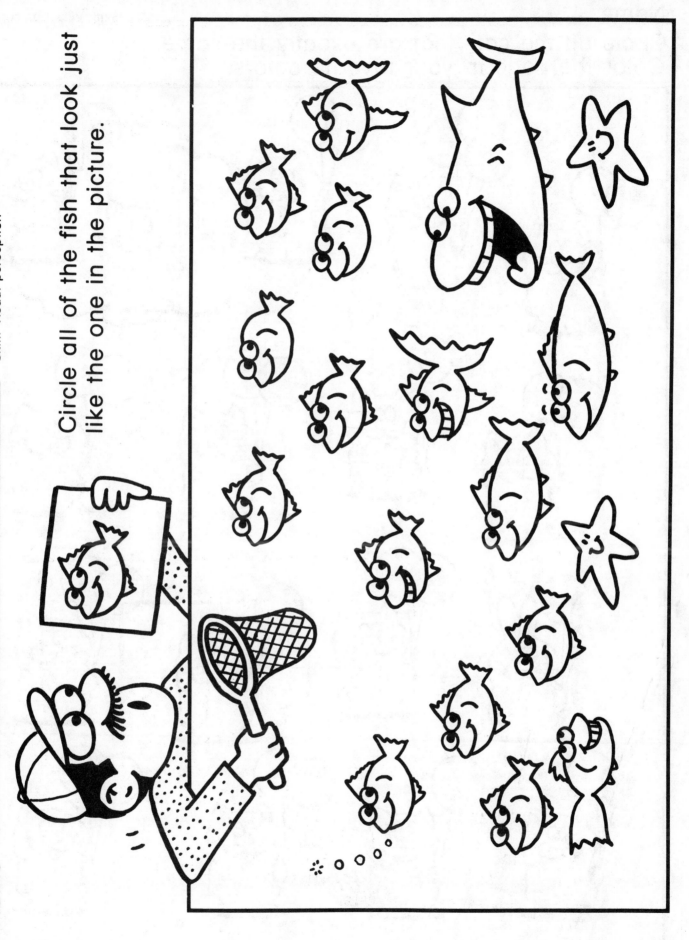

39

Name _____

Circle all the cats that are exactly the same.
Color the page in your favorite colors.

Name _____

Follow the path to the bear family.

Name _____

Follow the pattern.
Finish each row.

FS-2651   Pre-School Workbook-Book One

Skill: Eye-hand coordination

Finish each twin and color.

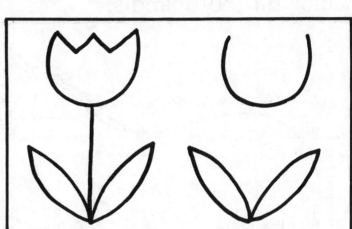

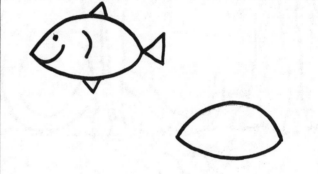

FS-2651   Pre-School Workbook-Book One

Name _____

Draw a line from each mother to her baby.
Color all the animals.

Name _____

Trace over the .... lines.
Color the picture.

Trace over the shapes.
Can you guess what they are?

H H H H H

C C C C C

A A A A A

D D D D D

F F F F F

L L L L L

Name _____

Trace over the _ _ _ lines. Color the picture.

47

Draw a line to the right baby. Color the animals.

FS-2651   Pre-School Workbook-Book One